TOPIC BOX

Fairs and Circuses

Pam Robson

Wayland

Titles in this series
Castles
Dinosaurs
Fairs and Circuses
Houses and Homes
Minibeasts
My Body
The Seasons
Transport

This book was prepared for Wayland (Publishers) Ltd
by Globe Education, Nantwich, Cheshire

Design concept by Pinpoint
Book design by Stephen Wheele Design
Artwork by Helen Smith

First published in 1995 by
Wayland (Publishers) Ltd
61 Western Road, Hove
East Sussex BN3 1JD

Printed and bound in Italy by
L. E. G. O. S.p.A., Vincenza

British Library Cataloguing in Publication Data

Robson, Pam
Fairs and Circuses. – (Topic Box Series)
I. Title II. Series
791

ISBN 0 7502 1467 8

Picture acknowledgements
British Museum 7l (Copyright British Museum)
Rex Features 4-5 (Barry Norman), 9 (Peter Brooker), 16, 17, 18, 19 (Dave Lewis), 20-21 (Wil Blanche),
21 (Nick Bailey), 22 (and back cover), 23 (Peter Brooker), 25l (Wil Blanche), 25r (and title page)
Robert Harding 27t (and front cover), 27b (N Boyd)
Spectrum 12 (Gunther Becker)
Wayland Picture Library 11
Zefa 7r

Contents

Fun Times

Have you ever enjoyed a day out at a funfair? In the tenth century, people lived in small towns and villages. They had no television or radio and no funfairs.

Travelling players moved from village to village. They brought news, told stories and amused people.

In the nineteenth century, fairs and circuses travelled the countryside bringing excitement into people's lives.

pipe and drum

harp

lute

Travelling players had simple musical instruments such as pipes, drums, harps and lutes.

4

(Left) Funfairs are exciting places, at night.

(Below) Performers often paraded through the streets when the circus arrived in town.

5

Ancient Times

The circus began long ago when the city of Rome was the centre of the Roman Empire. There was a big arena called the Circus Maximus. People loved to go there to watch games.

Races with horses and chariots were very popular. Teams would gallop seven times around the track.

There were also fights between armed men known as gladiators. They even fought wild animals.

Fights between gladiators and lions or tigers were popular.

6

Roman chariots raced at great speed pulled by four horses.

(Below) Gladiators wore iron helmets for protection.

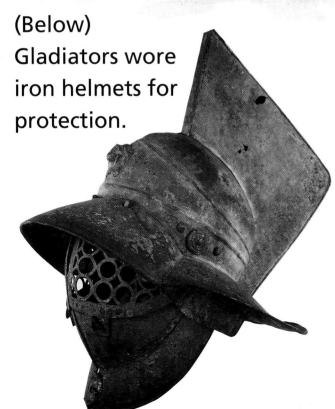

The Roman arena (above) is at Nîmes in France. Here thousands of people watched chariot races and gladiator contests.

Travelling Players

In the Middle Ages, entertainers travelled from village to village. There were jugglers and acrobats and people who played musical instruments, sang and told stories.

We still have travelling entertainers in our streets today. They play music and perform tricks for anyone who will stop to watch and listen.

Even our pop stars go from city to city giving concerts.

(Right) Street performers can be seen in many towns and cities.

(Below) In the Middle Ages, travelling players gathered whenever there was a fair.

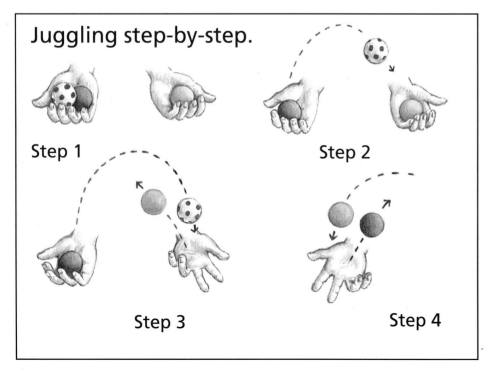

Juggling step-by-step.

Step 1

Step 2

Step 3

Step 4

The First Fairs

The first fairs were like markets. Traders came from distant places and people gathered around to buy their goods. The travelling players came along to entertain everyone.

Special permission was needed to hold a fair. This was known as its charter.

Some fairs traded in animals. Others were good for hiring labourers. Some became famous like St Bartholemew's Fair in London.

(Below) Farm workers in the Middle Ages went to a hiring fair to find work.

woodsman   shepherd

labourer   reaper

10

(Below) In cold winters, the River Thames sometimes froze hard. Frost fairs were held for weeks on end.

At a fair, goods like silks and carpets from far-off lands were for sale.

Bring on the Clowns

Clowning began with the travelling players who played funny tricks to make people laugh. As time went by these jesters joined first the fairs and then the circuses.

Clowns with white faces are known as Joeys after a famous clown called Joe Grimaldi. Clowns who wear baggy trousers and funny hats are known as Augustes. Clowns are not always men. Sometimes they are women.

The first clowns were jesters employed by rich lords in the Middle Ages.

Each clown has his or her own style of face painting. No clown ever copies another.

Auguste wears baggy trousers and a funny hat. Joey has a white face and wears a fancy suit.

Joey

Auguste

Father of the Circus

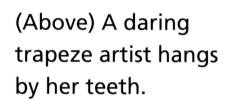

About 200 years ago, trick riding was very popular. A one-time cavalry officer, Philip Astley, gave riding shows in London. He discovered he could perform best in a ring that was 42 feet (12·8 m) across. Circus rings were always this size. Bigger circuses had two or three rings.

Astley took his circus to many countries and built a circus theatre in Paris. In America, Barnum and Bailey's circus became very famous.

(Above) A daring trapeze artist hangs by her teeth.

(Left) A tightrope walker balances on a rope.

A circus with its 'big top'.

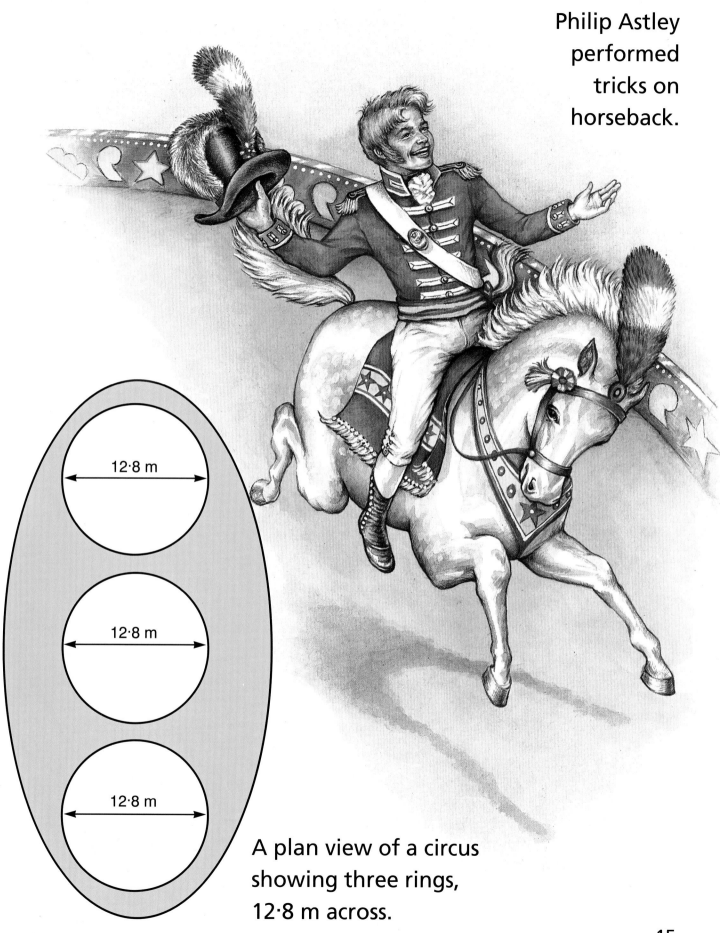

Philip Astley performed tricks on horseback.

12·8 m

12·8 m

12·8 m

A plan view of a circus showing three rings, 12·8 m across.

Performing Animals

People are fascinated by unusual animals. Long ago, wild animals drew the crowds in Ancient Rome. Travelling players sometimes had monkeys or dancing bears and all circuses had performing animals.

Some animals, like dogs, do seem to enjoy showing off and playing tricks, but most animals seem unhappy. Today, many people object if performing animals are used as entertainment.

(Left) The horses at the Spanish Riding School in Vienna are trained to perform spectacular tricks.

(Below)
"The animals are king"
at Jean Richard's circus –
a poster advertising
a French circus.

Les
ANIMAUX
sont
ROIS
AU CIRQUE
JEAN RICHARD

(Above) An
elephant
act in
a circus.

(Left) At fairs in
the Middle Ages,
dancing bears
were quite
common.

Circuses Today

In our world of video and television, only a few travelling circuses remain. These have become spectacular entertainments involving people rather than animals.

Television also uses circus ideas to make popular, entertaining programmes involving athletic contests between the home team and the contestants.

(Left) One of the exciting acts from the Circus Archaos.

(Left) Acrobats at the Circus du Soleil.

(Left) A team member of the television programme, Gladiators, swings into action against a contestant.

(Right) Circus performers must be very fit. They need to practise daily.

Travelling Fairs

As more railway lines were built, towns began to grow bigger and many of the old trade fairs disappeared.

Instead there were travelling funfairs. These set up for a week in one town and then moved on to the next. Roundabouts and sideshows were popular.

When the fairs moved on, the rides and fairground stands were taken apart and packed into trucks.

A nineteenth century traction engine hauling 40 tonnes of fairground equipment.

Dodgems (right) are a popular fairground ride.

(Below) A typical fairground layout.

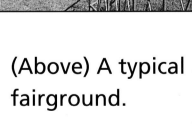

(Above) A typical fairground.

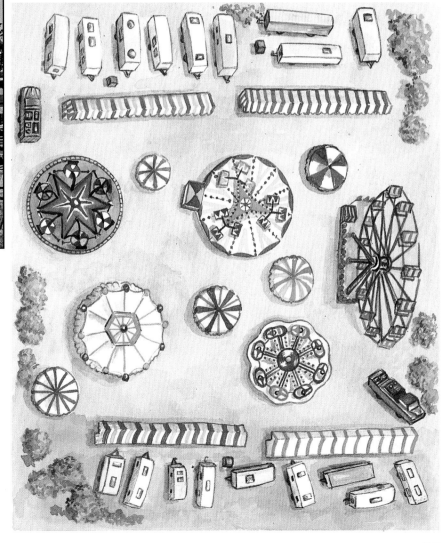

Roundabouts

The first fairground roundabouts were known as carousels. They had beautifully carved animals that glided up and down. The carousel was driven by a steam engine and music played on a steam organ as it turned.

Today, roundabouts are run by electricity and the rides are usually model cars, planes or rockets. Other roundabouts spin around or jolt up and down. The music is electronic.

A modern roundabout.

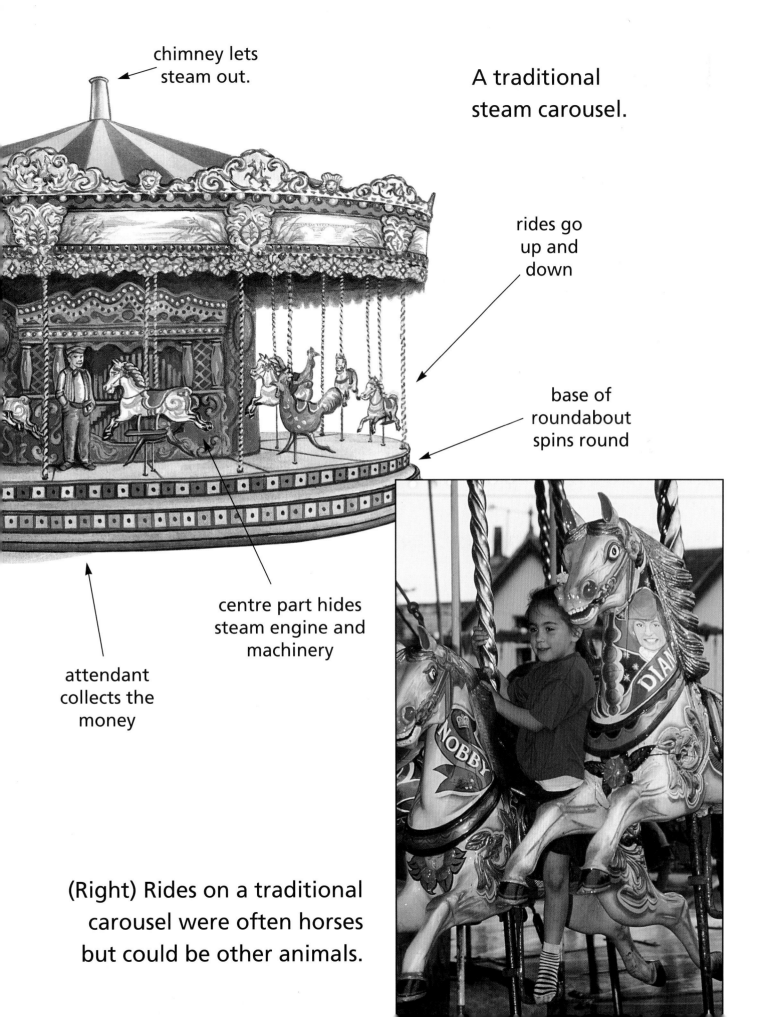

chimney lets
steam out.

A traditional
steam carousel.

rides go
up and
down

base of
roundabout
spins round

centre part hides
steam engine and
machinery

attendant
collects the
money

NOBBY

DIAN

(Right) Rides on a traditional
carousel were often horses
but could be other animals.

Big Wheels

People began to invent bigger and more thrilling rides. About 100 years ago George Ferris built a big wheel in Chicago in the United States.

Seats hung from the rim of the wheel. As the wheel turned you were first lifted high in the sky. Then you swung down towards the ground again, only to be lifted up high once more.

Nearly every funfair today has a Ferris wheel.

At the centre, a Ferris wheel is like a bicycle wheel.

ball bearings stop the weight of the wheel from crushing the axle

Ferris wheels must be very strong. This picture shows the structure of the base without the wheel.

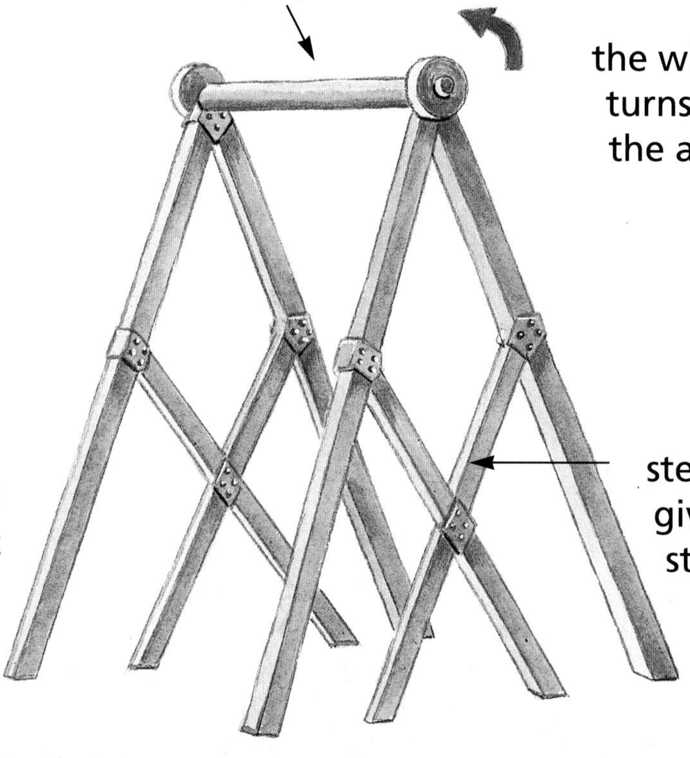

axle

the wheel turns on the axle

strong steel legs carry the weight of the wheels

steel struts give extra strength

(Left)
A Ferris wheel.

(Below) At a fair there are many different kinds of breathtaking rides that spin around.

Fairground Food

From earliest times, food was sold at fairs. Sometimes a whole ox was roasted on a spit over an open fire.

As the years passed, toffee apples, rock, doughnuts and candy floss became traditional. Today, people enjoy hamburgers and hot dogs.

The smell of food mixed with the sound of music and the humming of machinery is part of what makes a fairground such an exciting place.

In the Middle Ages, there was often a whole ox roasting over an open fire.

(Right) Fairings were small things like coloured ribbons, toffee apples and special gingerbread.

(Above) Candyfloss is like cotton wool made from sugar.

Today, fairground food is sold from vans that open up to make a small kitchen and a counter. They sell a whole range of foods from ice cream to chips and beefburgers.

Theme Parks

Today, more people have time
for fun than ever before.

Many countries have huge
permanent funfairs known as
theme parks. The most famous
are Disneyland, Disney World
and Disneyland Paris.

Theme parks have many
exciting and breathtaking
experiences. People go
there for a whole day
of fun.

29

Word List

Acrobat An entertainer who performs acts requiring skill, agility and co-ordination.

Arena An area, usually circular and surrounded by seats, in which entertainments take place.

Auguste A clown with distinctive face make-up who wears baggy trousers and a funny hat.

Chariot A two-wheeled, horse-drawn vehicle used in races in ancient times.

Circus Maximus An entertainment in Roman times where chariots raced 7 times around an oval track with a central barrier.

Dodgems Fairground cars with rubber bumpers which are designed to bump into each other in safety.

Fairings Presents collected in a fairground.

Ferris Wheel An enormous, vertically-rotating wheel with seats for passengers suspended from the rim. Invented by the American engineer, George Ferris (1859-96).

Frost Fair A fair held on the River Thames when it froze over during harsh winters in the sixteenth to nineteenth centuries.

Gladiators Slaves, prisoners or professional men trained as fighters in ancient Rome. Each type of gladiator wore distinctive armour. Gladiators called retiarri fought armed with nets and tridents.

Harp An ancient muscial instrument with vertical strings played by plucking with the fingers.

Hiring fair A special fair where servants and labourers put themselves up for hire. Those seeking work wore or carried an appropriate symbol for their labour.

Joey A clown wearing white face make-up named after Joe Grimaldi (1779-1837). He was the original white-faced clown who appeared in a spangled costume in pantomime at the Drury Lane theatre in London about 200 years ago.

Juggler An entertainer who throws and catches a number of similar objects in a sequence that has most of them in the air at the same time.

Lute An ancient pear-shaped, stringed musical instrument with a long 'neck' which was played by plucking the strings.

Sideshow An entertainment offered on the outskirts of a fair or circus. Sideshows are often stalls offering prizes for achieving high scores by throwing such things as darts, coconuts or ping-pong balls.

Theme park A permanent amusement park or funfair.

Traction engine A steam or diesel engine used to haul heavy loads along roads or over rough ground.

Finding Out More

Places to Visit

Bethnal Green Museum
of Childhood,
Cambridge Heath Road,
London, E2 9PA

British Museum,
Great Russell Street,
London, WC1

Hollycombe Steam
Collection, Liphook,
Hampshire

Museum of London,
150 London Wall,
London EC2Y 5HN

Theatre Museum,
Russell Street,
Covent Garden,
London, WC2 7PA

Tom Varley's Museum
of Steam,
Todber Caravan Park,
Gisburn,
Clitheroe,
Lancashire

Books to Read

A Circus Child, Jose
Patterson, (Hamish
Hamilton, 1986)

Fair Enough?, Jim Golland,
(Herga Press, 1993)

Fairground Family, Mog
Johnstone, (A & C Black,
1985)

Fairs and Circuses, Miriam
Moss, (Wayland, 1987)

Going to the Fair, Gill
Tanner, (A & C Black,
1992)

The Theatre Museum,
Alexander Schouvaloff,
(Scala Books, 1987)

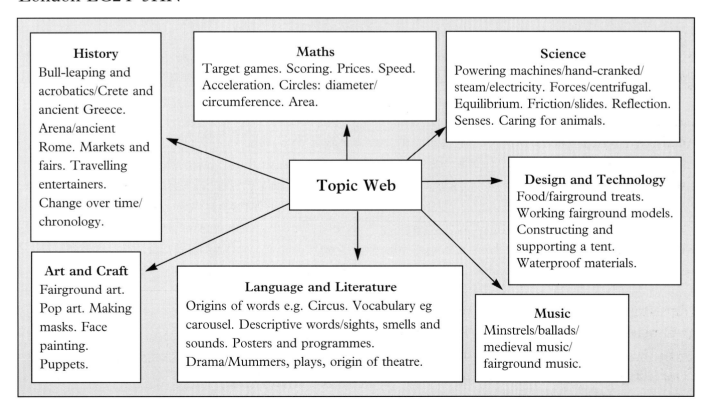

History
Bull-leaping and acrobatics/Crete and ancient Greece. Arena/ancient Rome. Markets and fairs. Travelling entertainers. Change over time/chronology.

Maths
Target games. Scoring. Prices. Speed. Acceleration. Circles: diameter/circumference. Area.

Science
Powering machines/hand-cranked/steam/electricity. Forces/centrifugal. Equilibrium. Friction/slides. Reflection. Senses. Caring for animals.

Topic Web

Design and Technology
Food/fairground treats. Working fairground models. Constructing and supporting a tent. Waterproof materials.

Art and Craft
Fairground art. Pop art. Making masks. Face painting. Puppets.

Language and Literature
Origins of words e.g. Circus. Vocabulary eg carousel. Descriptive words/sights, smells and sounds. Posters and programmes. Drama/Mummers, plays, origin of theatre.

Music
Minstrels/ballads/medieval music/fairground music.

Index